DRESS SENSE

CLOTHES OF THE ANCIENT WORLD

CHRISTINE HATT

Illustrated by JANE TATTERSFIELD

PETER BEDRICK BOOKS
NTC/Contemporary Publishing Group

Library of Congress Cataloging-in-Publication Data
is on file with the publisher.

First published in the United States in 2001 by
Peter Bedrick Books
A division of NTC/Contemporary Publishing Group
4255 West Touhy Avenue, Lincolnwood (Chicago) Illinois
60712-1975 U.S.A.

Published in the United Kingdom in 2000 by
Belitha Press Limited, London House,
Great Eastern Wharf, Parkgate Road,
London SW11 4NQ

Printed in Singapore
International Standard Book Number: 0-87226-670-2

Series editor: Claire Edwards
Series designer: Angie Allison
Picture researcher: Diana Morris
Consultant clothing historian: Dr. Jane Bridgeman
Education consultant: Anne Washtell

10 9 8 7 6 5 4 3 2 1

Picture acknowledgments:
Acropolis Museum, Athens/Werner Forman Archive: 6b. David
Bernstein Fine Art, NY/Werner Forman Archive: 7r. British
Museum/Werner Forman Archive: 6t. V&A Picture Library: 7t.

The artwork of the High Priest on page 16 is based on a drawing
by Barbara Phillipson, copied with permission from Alfred
Rubens, *A History of Jewish Costume*, published by Weidenfeld and
Nicolson 1967.

**The cover picture shows an ancient Greek woman
wearing a *peplos* tunic and *stephane* headdress.**

CONTENTS

Introduction 4

How We Know 6

Prehistoric Clothing 8

Mesopotamia 10

Ancient Egypt 12

Pharaohs and Queens 14

Hebrews 16

Persia 18

Crete and Mycenae 20

Ancient Greece 22

Ancient Greek Actors and Soldiers 24

Ancient Rome 26

Soldiers in Ancient Rome 28

The Celts 30

The Migrating Tribes 32

Ancient India and Pakistan 34

Ancient China 36

The Ancient Americas 38

Material Matters 40

Ancient Accessories 42

Maps of the Ancient World 44

Glossary 46

Index 48

Words in **bold** are explained in the glossary.

INTRODUCTION

This book will show you the clothes that people from many different lands wore in the ancient world. This period began thousands of years ago in prehistoric times. It continued through the rise, rule and fall of the first great civilizations around the world. It ended in about 500 AD, as the **Roman Empire** collapsed in the West.

Why wear clothes?

No one knows exactly why or when people began to wear clothes. The most obvious reason for covering the body is to protect it from the weather. Early humans probably started to cover themselves in furs to keep out the cold of the **Ice Age**. But even in hot places, such as Africa, **prehistoric** people often wore some clothing. This may have been to protect themselves from insects, thorny plants, or rough rocks. But many experts believe that men and women of the distant past did not dress for practical purposes alone.

Looking good

People who study the history of clothing have suggested three other main reasons why the earliest humans wore clothes—status, religion and appearance. Garments may have shown a person's status, for example as a member of a group or tribe. During religious ceremonies, people may have worn special clothes. They probably believed these clothes would give them magical powers (see page 9). Then as now, humans may simply have wanted to look good, either for their own pleasure or to attract a partner.

Early prehistoric people dressed in furs and skins. This archer's skirtlike loincloth is made from a single fur. The fur's ragged ends show that it has not been cut to fit, but left in its natural shape.

This prehistoric man is wearing an animal fur "skirt." The animal's tail can be seen at the front. The skirt is held up at the waist by leather strips.

The *toga picta*, made of gold-embroidered purple cloth, was worn in Roman times. At first it was the costume of victorious generals. Later it was worn by emperors (above) and consuls.

Robes of rank

As civilizations developed, clothing became a common way of showing someone's **rank** and wealth. Rulers wore splendid robes in fabrics that ordinary people could not afford. Members of important professions, such as priests, dressed in special costumes to make their status clear. Most civilizations also had armies, which led to the development of uniforms. Soldiers could be instantly recognized in a uniform, and this also helped them to bond with one another to create strong fighting units.

About this book

The next two pages will show you how experts have discovered what ancient people wore. Each double page that follows describes the clothing of a particular place and time. Material Matters boxes give more information on types of material from which clothes were made. Other boxes give information on special subjects, such as military or religious costumes. There is a brief time line at the top of each page, and maps on pages 44–45 will help you find some of the places mentioned in this book.

The royal bodyguards of the ancient Persian Empire were known as the Immortal Archers. They wore loose, embroidered tunics with flared sleeves, and probably close-fitting tunics underneath.

What is a costume?

A garment is an individual item of clothing. A costume is a set of clothes designed to be worn together.

Date fact

Some of the dates in this book have a *c.* in front of them. This stands for the Latin word *circa* and means "about."

A Matter of Modesty

Today, one of the main reasons for wearing clothes is modesty. Even on the beach in hot weather most people still wear swimsuits. But many ancient people did not worry about nudity. For example, Greek athletes did not wear clothes, even when taking part in public events such as the Olympic Games. Modesty became more important after the rise of Christianity in the first century AD and of Islam in the seventh century.

HOW WE KNOW

The study of early clothing is very difficult, because so few garments have survived from the ancient world. But experts look at those that do exist, as well as other evidence such as paintings, sculptures and written descriptions. In this way they can gradually build up fairly accurate pictures of what humans wore many thousands of years ago.

Greek statues were often very detailed. This one was made in the sixth century BC. You can see the folds in the woman's *peplos* dress and the curls in her hairstyle. Objects like this help experts find out what people wore in the past.

This ancient Egyptian tomb painting is more than 3,500 years old. It shows the fine linen garments and jeweled collars worn by a man called Nebamun, his wife and their daughter (the small figure at the front of the picture).

Ancient garments

Clothing materials usually fall to pieces as time passes. However, extremely dry, cold or wet conditions can preserve them. **Archaeologists** have found fragments of ancient textiles and even whole garments in hot, dry deserts, frozen **steppes** and wet bogs. Among them are linen clothes from Egypt, cotton clothes from Peru and woolen clothes from Denmark. Often these clothes had been buried in graves alongside their owners.

Ancient art

Ancient art of all sorts can give us valuable information about clothing. Experts can study Egyptian tomb paintings, Greek vases, Roman sculptures and Maya pots. Tiny wooden statues from ancient Chinese tombs are often clothed in miniature silk costumes. Small **terra-cotta** statues from ancient Greece may also show the shape and detail of clothing, but not the colors. Coins and **seals** may carry pictures of richly dressed rulers.

This museum conservator is carefully repairing a child's dress.

Looking at the evidence

Costume experts have to be careful when they study art evidence. There are several reasons for this. First, ancient art usually shows rich people, so it may tell us little about what ordinary people wore. Second, early artists often drew an ideal world. For example, many Egyptian tomb paintings show people dressed for the afterlife, not daily life. Lastly, some civilizations had strict, unchanging rules about how to draw humans. So artists may have shown them in clothes that were in fact long out of date.

Written sources

Costume experts also learn about what people wore by studying books and other written sources. But records from the ancient world are patchy. For example, the historians, novelists and poets of ancient Greece and ancient Rome often mention clothes, but they rarely describe them in much detail.

MATERIAL MATTERS

Experts in the USA examined the wrappings around a 2,000-year-old Egyptian mummy. They discovered that the inner wrappings were linen and the outer wrappings ramie, a fabric made from nettles. It is difficult for insects to eat through ramie, so this material was ideal for protecting the mummy.

Costume Care

Ancient costumes are precious. After archaeologists have studied them under microscopes and carried out chemical tests, they are cared for by **conservators**. Their job is to make sure that the clothes do not crumble or fade. They may add backing material to textiles to hold them together. They may treat them with chemicals to stop insects from eating them. They also make sure that the heating, lighting and air conditioning in museum rooms do not damage the garments.

This piece of cloth was made by people of the Paracas culture, who lived in Peru between about 600 and 200 BC. They embroidered garments with brightly dyed llama and alpaca wool.

PREHISTORIC CLOTHING

Early humans spread across the world during the last **Ice Age**, when ice sheets covered much of northern Europe, North America and other areas. **Prehistoric** people in cold places may have begun to dress in furs over 40,000 years ago.

To prepare animal hides for clothing, prehistoric people first pegged them firmly out on the ground. This stretched the hides and stopped them from moving around while the fur and flesh were removed.

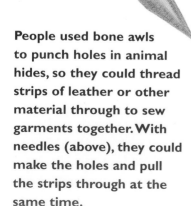

First furs

In Europe, people often wore bear and reindeer furs. They tied them on or held them in place with thorn shoulder pins and leather waist thongs. In North America, people dressed in the furs of buffalo, and later deer and beaver.

This picture shows an 8,000-year-old pair of moccasins. They are made of antelope hide and were found in Danger Cave, Utah.

Preparing hides

Humans slowly invented ways to make the hard animal **hides** soft and waterproof, such as by rubbing them with fish oil or egg yolk, or a solution of oak-tree bark. They removed the fur by scraping it off with **flints** or by dissolving it with **alkaline** substances such as ashes.

Successful sewing

Humans also learned how to cut the hides into shapes to fit the body, and to sew the pieces together into garments. In northern Europe, they sewed with needles made of bone, horn or **ivory**, while in North America, bone **awls** were used. For thread they used leather thongs, animal **sinews** or tough plant fibers.

People used bone awls to punch holes in animal hides, so they could thread strips of leather or other material through to sew garments together. With needles (above), they could make the holes and pull the strips through at the same time.

Textile traditions

Farming first developed in the Middle East, and people soon began to make fabrics from farmed plants and animal hair. Linen, made from **flax**, may be the oldest fabric. Pieces more than 8,000 years old have been found in Israel. **Archaeologist**s have also found 5,000-year-old woolen cloth in Egypt, and cotton fabric of a similar age in Pakistan.

This woolen shirt was made in Sweden during the Bronze Age. It has embroidery on the sleeves and around the neck.

MATERIAL MATTERS

The oldest known piece of felt was discovered in the village of Çatal Hüyük, Turkey. It is more than 7,000 years old. Felt is made by pressing, heating and wetting tightly rolled fur so that the hairs tangle and weave together. Felt was made in central Asia during the prehistoric era, and Mongolians who live there now still make it in the same way.

Ritual Dress

Ancient paintings on cave walls, for example in France and Spain, sometimes show people wearing antlers (see right), horses' tails and masks, as well as animal skins. These prehistoric humans may have dressed in special garments to take part in religious rituals. By wearing something taken from an animal, they may have hoped to gain its strength, or the ability to hunt the animal successfully. Such ceremonies have taken place for at least 35,000 years.

SKINS FOR ALL SEASONS FROM c. 40,000 BC

Many of the garments made in Ice Age Europe were similar to suits worn by **Inuit** people in Canada today. People wore thick fur boots, pants and long-sleeved tunics, usually with a hood (see left). These were sewn together with reindeer sinews using needles made from reindeer horn. Some had bone buttons. In warmer parts of the world, people dressed in skin loincloths or skirts, or pants and sleeveless tunics (see right). These garments were sometimes decorated with shells. People also wore necklaces and other jewelry made of animal teeth, ivory or **amber**.

c. 4000 BC
Rise of Sumerian civilization.

c. 2000 BC
Rise of Babylonian civilization in southern Mesopotamia.
Rise of Assyrian civilization in northern Mesopotamia.

c. 1700 BC
Babylonian Empire at height of its power.

MESOPOTAMIA

Mesopotamia was the area of the Middle East between the Tigris and Euphrates rivers. This is where modern Iraq now lies. Several of the world's earliest civilizations grew up in the region, and their peoples gradually developed many distinctive styles of costume.

Sumerian skins

The first of these civilizations was the Sumerian, which began in about 4000 BC. Its early people dressed in skirts made of sheepskins. They also wore short skin cloaks. In about 3000 BC the Sumerians began to weave wool into a cloth to which they attached tufts of animal hair. This cloth, called *kaunakès*, was made into skirts and full-length cloaks. Later in the Sumerian period, people wore long, draped wool and linen garments with tasseled edges.

Babylonian costumes

From about 1700 BC on, the **empire** of the Babylonians became the most important in Mesopotamia. The people wore two main items of clothing—a full-length, short-sleeved tunic and a fringed shawl draped over the top. These garments were often made of fine wool and dyed bright colors. Patterns were sometimes embroidered onto the cloth. In the late years of the empire, men wore tunics alone, with long sleeves and neck tassels.

Assyrian gold

The Mesopotamian empire of Assyria reached the height of its power in about 750 BC. Its people wore similar clothes to the Babylonians. Assyrians were very fond of jewelry—both men and women wore heavy gold earrings, bracelets and "dog collar" necklaces. Slaves shielded rich women from the sun with parasols.

A Sumerian man wearing a wraparound *kaunakès* skirt. These garments sometimes had long tails of fabric attached at the back.

The kings of Babylon sometimes wore this decorative style of headdress with feathers around the top.

This bracelet was found inside a royal tomb in a city called Kalhu, once the capital of Assyria. It is made of gold with pieces of turquoise-colored enamel set in it, and has an agate gemstone in the center.

The Babylonians usually wore leather sandals on their feet. Most styles covered the heel at the back and held the big toe in a ring.

ASSYRIAN SPLENDOR
C. EIGHTH CENTURY BC

The Assyrian king on the left is dressed in a short-sleeved tunic with a long shawl wound around his body to make a double-fringed skirt. Only the king was allowed to wear the shawl in this way. Like all Assyrian men, kings took great care of their hair and beards. They often darkened them with black dye and curled them with hot irons. Sometimes they also wore wigs. The king's tasseled headdress is called a miter.

The Assyrian queen on the right wears a fringed robe with a circle pattern over a white linen tunic. Her accessories include a gold crown and large gold earrings.

Army Outfits

The uniforms of the Assyrian army developed over time. At first, soldiers on foot and horseback dressed in short fabric tunics, belted at the waist. Later, they wore breast- and backplates (see right) or knee-length tunics made of metal for extra protection. Archers in chariots or on horseback often wore full-length tunics covered in metal plates. Conical metal helmets with cheek-flaps protected soldiers' heads.

MATERIAL MATTERS

Kaunakès cloth (see page 10) was covered in tufts of animal hair. These were often arranged in decorative layers and combed to look neat. *Kaunakès* was sometimes also made by weaving loops into the cloth rather than sewing tufts on afterward. The aim was to make a material that looked like sheep or goatskin, but that was easier to shape and wear.

c. 5000 BC
Ancient Egyptian civilization begins to develop.

c. 3100 BC
Kingdoms of Upper and Lower Egypt united.

c. 2686–2181 BC
Old Kingdom

c. 2181–1991 BC
First Intermediate Period

ANCIENT EGYPT

Egypt became a powerful, united kingdom in about 3100 BC, and its civilization lasted for almost 3,000 years. The people of this hot, dry, desert land wore light garments. Clothing styles changed little during this long period of history.

Early styles

The history of ancient Egypt is divided into three main periods, the Old, Middle and New Kingdoms. The Old Kingdom lasted from about 2686 to 2181 BC. At this time many working men wore very little. The main items of clothing were loincloths or short **kilts**, made of rough, unbleached linen. Nobles wore longer kilts of finer linen, some pleated at the front. Styles changed little in the Middle Kingdom (1991–1786 BC), but some nobles began to wear kilts with skirts over the top.

This Old Kingdom noble is wearing a linen kilt with an overlapping pleated section. The end of this section is pulled through the linen belt around his waist to hold the kilt firmly in place.

New Kingdom novelties

Egyptian civilization reached its high point under the New Kingdom, from 1567 to 1085 BC. During this time, its rulers, called pharaohs, conquered nearby lands such as Phoenicia and Syria, and new clothing styles spread from there. Rich men began to wear long tunics and draped robes, either loose or belted. Kilts remained the standard garment for working men.

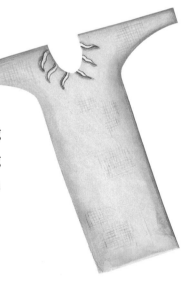

Rich Egyptians usually shaved their heads then put wigs made of human hair on top. This New Kingdom woman wears a long **lappet wig**. It is decorated with a headband made of gemstones set in a wire frame.

Women's wear

During the Old and Middle Kingdoms, women wore tight, straight sheath dresses and possibly also long-sleeved, V-necked dresses with tie fastenings at the neck. Sheath dresses remained popular in the New Kingdom. But many rich women began to wear robes made of two pieces of linen joined at the top, and **sari**like garments made of a single piece of fabric draped in a variety of ways.

Linen tunics like this were found in an Egyptian woman's tomb. Egyptians believed in life after death, and the tunics were probably made for her to wear then. Experts are not sure if women wore such tunics in real life.

MATERIAL MATTERS

Most ancient Egyptian clothes were made of linen, but animal hides were also popular for kilts, belts, shoes and sometimes gloves. In very early times, people wore raw skins. Then, gradually, they learned to make soft leather. At first, they spread salt and other minerals on the hides in a process called **tawing**. Later they buried the hides in pits with oak **galls**, oak bark and water. This **tanning** process took many months.

Priestly Costume

The priests of ancient Egypt dressed in tunics and kilts of bleached white linen, which were sometimes pleated. Some important priests draped leopard skins over their linen garments (see left). The leopards' heads, paws and tails were usually left on the **hides**. The priests may also have worn fabric that was painted or woven to look like leopard skin instead.

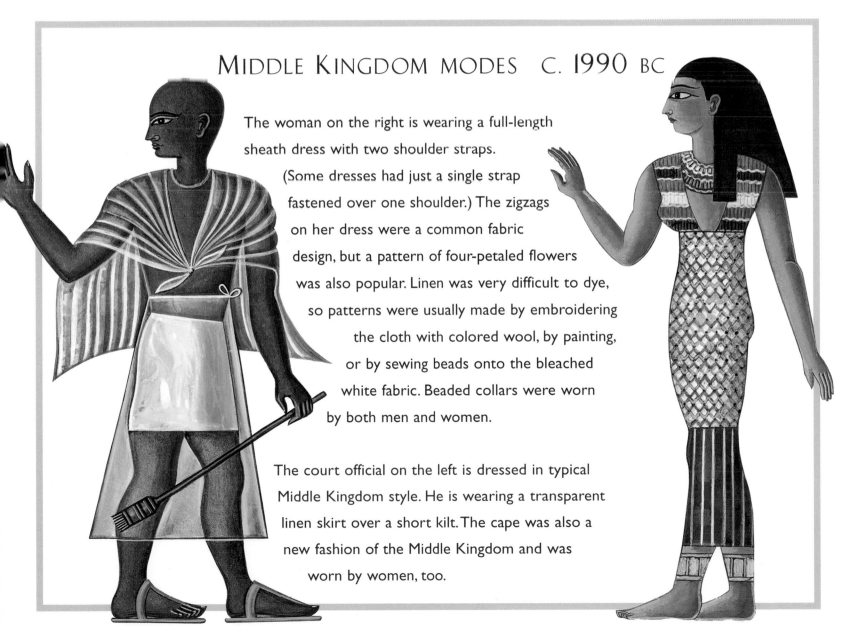

MIDDLE KINGDOM MODES c. 1990 BC

The woman on the right is wearing a full-length sheath dress with two shoulder straps. (Some dresses had just a single strap fastened over one shoulder.) The zigzags on her dress were a common fabric design, but a pattern of four-petaled flowers was also popular. Linen was very difficult to dye, so patterns were usually made by embroidering the cloth with colored wool, by painting, or by sewing beads onto the bleached white fabric. Beaded collars were worn by both men and women.

The court official on the left is dressed in typical Middle Kingdom style. He is wearing a transparent linen skirt over a short kilt. The cape was also a new fashion of the Middle Kingdom and was worn by women, too.

13

PHARAOHS AND QUEENS

Ancient Egypt was ruled by kings called pharaohs. The special styles and fine fabrics of their costumes showed that they were the most important people in the kingdom. Their wives looked equally splendid.

Early outfits

The earliest pharaohs wore short, sleeveless tunics. Belts with jeweled **pendants** were fastened around the waist and bulls' or lions' tails attached at the back as a sign of royal power. In the Old Kingdom, pharaohs often wore grander versions of nobles' kilts. One type was made of pleated linen wound around the body to form three sections at the front. Another had a triangular **apron** decorated with royal symbols such as serpents.

New styles

Pharaohs' clothes did not change much during the Middle Kingdom, but their garments became more elaborate in the New Kingdom. Pharaohs of this era often wore long robes of transparent, pleated linen with short kilts underneath and jeweled aprons on top. Robes were sometimes draped to look like three separate garments— a **kilt**, tunic and cloak. Long, pleated kilts with low waists also became fashionable.

Queens' costumes

During the Old and Middle Kingdoms, queens often wore sheath dresses. In the New Kingdom, robes (see box right), **sari**like garments and long skirts with short capes were popular. Egyptian queens decorated their costumes with jewels, gold and embroidery. They also wore special royal headdresses, including one shaped like a vulture with its wings spreading down over the hair.

The regions of Upper and Lower Egypt were united in about 3100 BC (see page 12). Afterward, the pharaohs wore a double crown that combined Upper Egypt's white crown with Lower Egypt's red one.

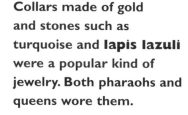

Collars made of gold and stones such as turquoise and **lapis lazuli** were a popular kind of jewelry. Both pharaohs and queens wore them.

Pharaohs and queens often wore thonged sandals made of braided leather or palm leaves. There were several different designs.

This early tunic is sleeveless and has a strip at the top that fastens over the left shoulder. The animal's tail at the back was a sign of the pharaoh's power. The pendants at the front were made of leather and precious stones.

ROYAL ROBES C. 1320 BC

This couple are the New Kingdom pharaoh Tutankhamun and his wife Ankhesenamun. Tutankhamun is wearing a pleated linen kilt in the low-waistline style. A decorative belt with pendant apron and streamers holds the kilt in place. He has a large, jeweled collar around his neck, and on his head he wears a ceremonial headdress and a curled wig.

Ankhesenamun's robe is made from two pieces of fabric joined at the top. The piece at the back is pulled forward and tied in a knot over the piece at the front. Decorated streamers fall from the knot. Like her husband, the queen also wears a collar, wig and elaborate headdress. Her eyes are outlined with black paint and colored with eye shadow.

Into Battle

Pharaohs often wore tight-fitting armored coats (see right) when they rode into battle on their war chariots. The coats were made of leather with protective metal or bone panels. On their heads they usually wore a crown known as a *khepresh*. This was decorated with a serpent at the front. The *khepresh* was often blue, but could also be red or white.

MATERIAL MATTERS

Pharaohs, queens and their people liked to wear linen garments for several reasons. First, it comes from **flax**, which is a plant. This meant that it was not considered unclean like wool, which comes from an animal. Second, it was white, a color that Egyptians believed to be sacred. Also, linen was cool to wear and easy to wash.

15

THE HEBREWS

The Hebrews were an ancient people of the Middle East. Their early history is told in the **Old Testament** of the Bible, but many details are unclear. Experts do know that by the eleventh century BC, they were living in a kingdom called Israel and were later conquered by the Assyrians. Early Hebrew dress was influenced by Assyrian and also Egyptian styles.

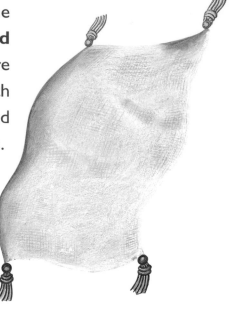

The clothes worn by the high priest of the Hebrews are described in the Bible. They included a long tunic, and a chest panel decorated with 12 gemstones. Each stone represented one of the tribes of Israel.

Problems of evidence

It is not easy to find out what the Hebrews wore. Costume descriptions in the Bible are difficult to understand. Religious laws did not allow people to make carvings of humans, and no other art has survived. Experts must look at images made by other peoples, such as the Egyptians and Assyrians. None survives from early times.

Early garments

The earliest Hebrews probably wore loincloths, skirts and shawls made from the **hides** of their sheep and goats. Gradually, they learned to spin and weave a kind of rough clothing fabric. By about 4,000 years ago, men and women were probably wearing long woolen tunics decorated with stripes or zigzags. They may have been woven from or embroidered with dyed wools from nearby Phoenicia.

Tunics and tassels

By about the eighth century BC, important men and women wore a full-length, sleeved tunic (*kethoneth*) with a fringed hem. A fringed cloak (*simla*) was wrapped over the top. Men may also have worn tasseled waist **girdles**. According to the Bible, the tassels (*tsitsith*) were to help the Hebrews remember God's commandments. In fact, Assyrians and others also wore tassels on their hems.

Hebrew men often attached *tsitsith*, fringed tassels, to their garments. By about the fifth century AD, cloaks with *tsitsith* at the corners had become special Jewish garments known as *talliths* (prayer shawls). Today, Jewish men still wear prayer shawls during religious services.

This mother-of-pearl shell from the Red Sea was once used to hold makeup. It was found in the Jewish royal palace and fortress of Masada, near the Dead Sea. It dates from the first century AD.

A pair of leather sandals was also discovered at Masada (see left). They were found near a female skeleton, so were probably worn by a Jewish woman nearly 2,000 years ago.

MATERIAL MATTERS

The Hebrews usually made their clothes from wool and linen. Religious laws did not allow them to weave the two into a single fabric, but they could be worn together in separate garments. Fabrics colored with bright dyes were very popular. Red dye was made from a type of plant called henna, and yellow was made from safflowers. The Hebrews also used wools that had been colored red, blue or purple using dyes from a type of shellfish called murex.

Greek Garments

By the first century AD, the kingdom of Israel had long ceased to exist, but Judaea had survived Persian and Greek rule to become part of the **Roman Empire**. Its people, now known as Jews, sometimes wore items of Persian clothing, such as trousers, but experts think that their everyday costume was based on Greek dress. Evidence for this comes from **frescoes** painted in a **synagogue** in Syria in the third century AD (see left). They show Jewish men wearing the Greek *chiton* tunic (see page 22). People also wore *himation* cloaks —Jesus wore one edged with *tsitsith* tassels.

CARVED IN STONE
NINTH TO EIGHTH CENTURY BC

The picture on the left is based on the earliest surviving image of an ancient Hebrew. The man is probably a king and appears on an Assyrian **obelisk** that dates from the ninth century BC. He is wearing a short-sleeved, full-length *kethoneth* tunic with fringing along the bottom. He has a girdle around his waist and a soft, pointed cap on his head.

The Assyrians conquered Israel in the eighth century BC. The image on the right is taken from a carving that shows Israelites captured by the Assyrians. The woman is wearing a long-sleeved, calf-length *kethoneth* with a *simla* cloak over the top. The cloak is pulled up over her head and covers her hair.

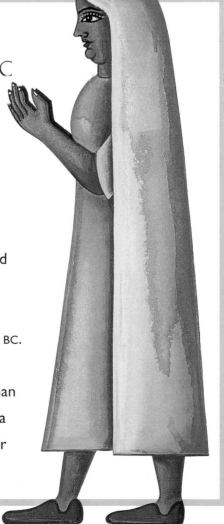

PERSIA

Ancient Persia covered roughly the area of the modern country Iran. In the sixth century BC, the Persians defeated the Babylonians to create a huge **empire** stretching from India in the east to Turkey in the west. Unlike earlier peoples in the region, the Persians mainly wore sewn, fitted clothes, rather than loose, draped robes.

Persian men often wore a type of hat known as a Phrygian cap. The caps were made of felt or leather and had a point at the top that drooped over to the front, back or side.

Trousers and tunics

The Persians' ancestors had been horse-riding **nomads** in the icy Asian **steppes**. They developed clothing that was warm and easy to wear in the saddle. Men wore trousers and knee-length tunics, often with a coat over the top. At first these garments were made from animal skins, but in Persia, people began to use wool, linen and, later, silk.

Flowing robes

The Persians adopted another item of clothing from the Medes, who lived in the same region. Many high-ranking Medes wore a long, draped garment similar to the Egyptian robe (see page 12). In Persia this garment was worn by the king. Trousers were often worn underneath.

The Persians wore various types of leather shoe. Some were tied tightly to the foot with laces (above). Others were fastened with buttons (see right).

Female fashions

Persian carvings and other art forms show mainly men, so it is difficult for experts to work out what women wore. In the early years of the empire, women probably dressed in short-sleeved tunics, large veils that covered their heads and shoulders, and perhaps also trousers. As time passed, women probably began to wear Assyrian-style clothing with their veils. Assyrian styles included fuller tunics with fringed shawls draped over the shoulder, around the waist or both. The most common fabric was linen.

Experts believe that Persian women often wore large, plain veils that covered their heads, shoulders and mouths.

A KING AND A RICH MAN
C. 500 BC

The picture on the left shows King Darius I, who ruled the Persian Empire from 521 to 486 BC. His full, brightly colored robe is patterned with rosettes and pulled tight around the waist with a jeweled belt. He wears tight, legging-style trousers underneath his robe and has buttoned leather shoes on his feet. Darius's crown is made of gold **inlaid** with jewels. It is perched on top of dark hair that has been curled into ringlets.

The man on the right is a rich Persian. His woolen trousers are close-fitting like leggings at the foot, but wider at the top. His short tunic is made of patterned wool and is belted around the waist. The coat reaches almost to the ground. The man's cap is made of felt and has streamers at the back.

War Wear

There were many types of Persian military uniform. **Cavalry** often wore plumed helmets with metal-plated tunics and fabric trousers. Foot soldiers wore colorful tunics with waist sashes and felt caps or fabric hats (see above). The best royal archers, called the Immortals, dressed in long, gold-embroidered tunics (see page 5). There are pictures of the Immortals on the walls of Emperor Darius's palace at Susa, once the capital of the Persian Empire.

MATERIAL MATTERS

Silk was originally produced in China, but knowledge of how to make it gradually spread along the **Silk Roads** (see page 37) to Persia. Brightly colored and patterned silks were woven by the Sassanians, who ruled Persia from the third century AD. These materials were highly valued in the West, and fragments of them have survived.

c. 3000 BC
Minoan civilization grows up on Crete.

c. 2000 BC
Palace of Knossos built.

c. 1600 BC
The Mycenaeans of eastern Greece come into contact with the Minoans.

CRETE AND MYCENAE

The first civilization in Europe was the Minoan civilization. It grew up on the Mediterranean island of Crete from about 3000 BC. The Minoans developed a unique, decorated style of costume. From about 1600 BC on, Greeks living in Mycenae on the nearby mainland came into contact with the Minoans and adopted their styles of dress.

Palace pictures

The best evidence for Minoan costume comes from **frescoes** and **terra-cotta** figurines. These have been discovered in the ruins of Cretan palaces such as Knossos. Most of the people shown are high-ranking members of society, priests or gods, so experts know more about their garments than the clothing of ordinary people.

Skirts and bodices

In the early years of Minoan civilization, women dressed in loincloths. As time passed these developed into long skirts, often with flounces, that curved out from belted waists. The skirts were made of linen, or from wool or leather dyed in bright colors such as purple and red. The fabric was often embroidered with patterns. Above their skirts, women wore tightly laced, short-sleeved **bodices**.

Minoan men

Minoan men dressed in loincloths made of wool, linen or leather. Some loincloths were in a **kilt** style—short at the back with a tasseled point at the front. Others were in a shorter **apron** style, which finished in a point at the back, or at the back and the front. Men wore cloth or leather belts decorated with gold, silver and other metals, often beaten into shapes such as spirals. The belts were pulled tight to emphasize the men's broad, muscular chests.

This Minoan man wears an apron-style loincloth with a point at the back and the front. He has a dagger tucked into the leather belt around his waist. The man is barefoot but has cloth strips wound around his legs.

This picture of a woman is based on a small statue of a Minoan goddess. Her skirt has six layers and a decorative apron over the top. Above the waist she wears a tight bodice.

Minoan men's sandals often had leather strips wound around the ankles. The rich sometimes decorated these with beads. In cold weather, men generally wore short leather boots instead.

c. 1400 BC
Eruption of a volcano on the island of Thera destroys the Minoan and probably the Mycenaean civilization.

c. 1400–800 BC
The Dark Age—Greece recovers from the volcanic eruption.

MATERIAL MATTERS

The Cretans were expert wool-weavers. A flock of about 80,000 sheep supplied fleeces for use in a major workshop at the palace of Knossos. There the wool was spun and colored with plant and animal dyes. It was then woven into fine fabrics for rich people's clothing.

Mycenaean Dress

Mycenaean Greek women often dressed in Minoan-style skirts and bodices. They also wore long tunics with short sleeves and belts around the waist. Mycenaean men often wore short tunics with leggings. Another popular fashion was shorts with a matching sleeveless top. Both shorts and top were decorated with tassels, tufts of animal hair or perhaps felt (see left).

CRETAN FINERY C. 1500 BC

The man on the left is dressed in a kilt-style loincloth made of embroidered linen. The leather belt is trimmed with gold, and the triangular tassel at the front is made of beads. The man's long, fringed hair and the **lapis lazuli** bracelets around his arm and ankles are all typically Minoan. Both men and women loved to adorn themselves with jewelery.

The woman on the right wears a flounced dress from the Late Minoan period. At this time a piece of light, see-through linen joined the two sides of the bodice at the front. This style was also popular in Mycenae. The woman's dark hair is very long and covered with a delicate pearl headdress.

ANCIENT GREECE

The Minoan civilization (see pages 20–21) was destroyed by a volcanic eruption in about 1400 BC. The Mycenaeans probably perished, too. But by about 900 BC Greece was slowly recovering, and in the early fifth century BC the Classical Period began. During this era, most people wore graceful, draped clothing.

This man is wearing a type of Doric *chiton* called an *exomis*. It is fastened on the left shoulder only, leaving the right shoulder uncovered. The *exomis* was worn by slaves and workers, not the rich.

The Doric *chiton*

The main item of clothing was the **chiton** (tunic). The simplest type was the Doric *chiton*. It was made of one or two lengths of woolen fabric pinned at the shoulder and belted at the waist. The men's tunic was short. The women's tunic, known as the *peplos*, was worn in various lengths, often on top of an Ionic *chiton* (see below). A special style of *peplos* was made by folding a piece of cloth to create a double layer at the top.

The Ionic *chiton*

The Ionic *chiton* became fashionable later than the Doric. It was made from a rectangle of linen or fine wool folded in half and sewn together down the long side. The fabric was pinned together on the shoulders, and folds of fabric were joined along the arms to create elbow-length sleeves. Women's Ionic *chitons* were full-length, men's usually knee-length. A single or double **girdle** held the *chiton* at the waist.

Greeks pinned their tunics and cloaks together with brooches called *fibulae*. Only a rich person could have afforded a *fibula* like this one, made of decorated gold.

Many Greek women kept themselves cool by waving small feathered fans (above) in front of their faces. Other women employed slaves to wave much larger fans for them. These fans were attached to long poles.

Classical cloaks

Men and women wore long, loose **himation** cloaks. Men often wound their cloaks over one shoulder and under the other. Women sometimes draped them over both shoulders and pulled up the back to cover their heads. Some people wore a short cloak called a *chlamys*.

Turning Heads

Women in Classical Greece usually wore their hair long and pulled into an elegant bun called a **chignon** at the back. Sometimes a length of hair was pulled out of the chignon to form a ponytail. The hair was often dyed blonde and decorated with ribbons. Women also wore many styles of headdress, including a crescent-shaped tiara called a *stephane* (see above). It was often joined to a linen bag that supported the chignon.

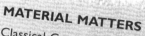

MATERIAL MATTERS

Classical Greek garments were made of wool, linen and sometimes cotton. Starch was used to produce fashionable, crinkled linen, or the crinkles were woven into the fabric itself. A shiny version of this material was made by working oil into the weave. Silk clothing was sometimes worn in this era (wild silk was made on the Greek island of Kos), but became more common later.

GRACEFUL GREEKS C. 450 BC

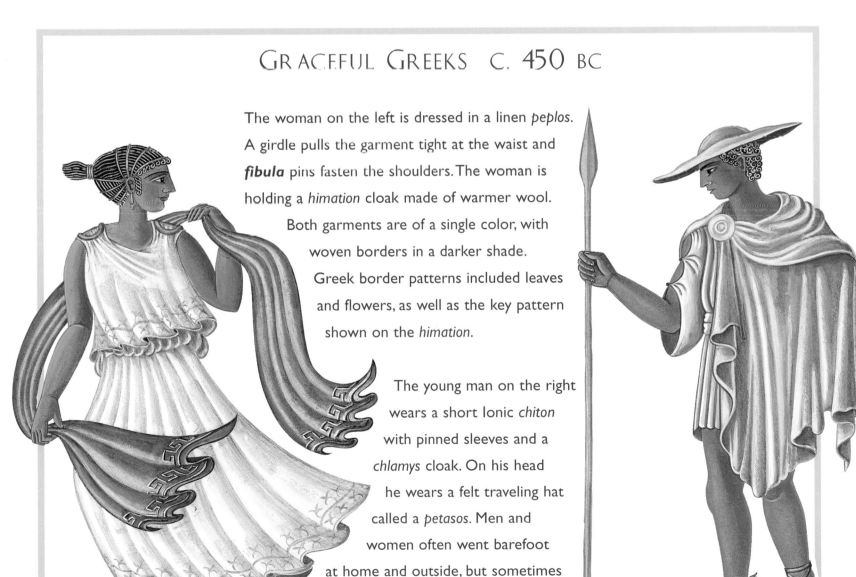

The woman on the left is dressed in a linen *peplos*. A girdle pulls the garment tight at the waist and **fibula** pins fasten the shoulders. The woman is holding a *himation* cloak made of warmer wool. Both garments are of a single color, with woven borders in a darker shade. Greek border patterns included leaves and flowers, as well as the key pattern shown on the *himation*.

The young man on the right wears a short Ionic *chiton* with pinned sleeves and a *chlamys* cloak. On his head he wears a felt traveling hat called a *petasos*. Men and women often went barefoot at home and outside, but sometimes wore strapped leather sandals.

23

ANCIENT GREEK ACTORS AND SOLDIERS

In ancient Greece, as in the modern world, people with special jobs often had special clothing. Soldiers dressed in armor, while actors wore costumes and masks that showed the type of character they were playing.

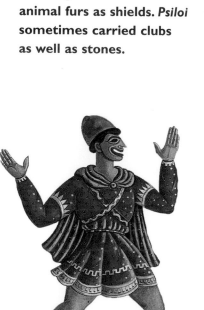

Stone-throwers called *psiloi* fought with the Greek army, but were not true soldiers. They wore ordinary clothes and used animal furs as shields. *Psiloi* sometimes carried clubs as well as stones.

Foot-soldier fashions

Greek foot soldiers of the Classical Period were called *hoplites*. They wore short **chitons** with armor on top. The armor had three main parts—a **cuirass** (breastplate and backplate), **greaves** (leg guards) and a helmet. The cuirass was made of shaped bronze, metal scales, leather or linen. The greaves and helmets were also made of bronze. Hoplites were named after the shields they carried, which were called *hoplons*.

Cavalry costume

The Greek **cavalry** dressed in *chitons* and cuirasses. They also had brimmed metal helmets and knee-length leather boots. They usually wore a bronze arm guard on one arm to fend off blows and carried a sword or spear with the other. Stone-throwers called *psiloi* also formed part of Greek armies. They held animal skins in front of themselves for protection.

Theatrical costume

The Greeks enjoyed going to the theater. All actors were men but they played male and female parts, changing character several times in a single play. Men who acted in tragedies often wore long, padded *chitons* in dark colors, and thick-soled boots to make themselves tall. Comic actors wore short *chitons* in bright colors or dressed up as animals. All actors wore masks. The masks showed who the characters were and what they felt.

A group of actors known as the chorus took part in most Greek plays. They all spoke together to comment on what the main actors were doing. This chorus member is dressed as a bird for a comedy play.

This actor is dressed as a soldier in a *chiton*, short *chlamys* cloak and mask. Even in tragedies, actors playing soldiers wore short *chitons*.

431–404 BC
Wars between the two Greek city-states of Athens and Sparta.

338 BC
King Philip II of Macedonia defeats Greek city-states.

FROM 336 BC
Philip's son Alexander the Great begins a campaign of expansion and creates a Greek Empire.

DRESSED FOR ACTION C. 450 BC

The hoplite on the left is wearing a bronze cuirass shaped to look like a man's chest muscles. Leather strips hang from the bottom and partly cover the skirt of the *chiton* underneath. Bronze greaves, also shaped like muscles, protect the hoplite's legs. His helmet has cheek guards and a horsehair crest. He carries a short iron sword and is holding a round bronze-and-leather shield called a *hoplon*.

The cavalryman on the right is wearing a *chiton*, metal cuirass, one full arm guard and a helmet. His *chlamys* cloak could be rolled up to give his arm extra protection. He is carrying a spear and has his sword in a **baldric**.

MATERIAL MATTERS

Greek actors' masks were usually made of cork or stiffened linen. Before masks were invented, the actors probably made up their faces with wine dregs or dangerous substances such as white lead.

Alexander's Armor

In 338 BC the Greek city-states were defeated by King Philip II, who ruled the nearby state of Macedonia. His son Alexander the Great went on to conquer the Persian Empire. During one battle against the Persians, Alexander wore a linen cuirass instead of his usual bronze one. The layers of linen were glued together to make the cloth stiff, so that it protected him from weapons. The cuirass was also light and allowed him to move easily. He decided never to wear a metal cuirass again. In battle, Alexander also always wore a Phrygian-style helmet (see left).

ANCIENT ROME

The Roman **republic** was founded in the sixth century BC. Its armies gradually conquered the rest of Italy, Greece, Egypt and other lands. In 27 BC, the republic became an **empire**, which lasted until 476 AD. Many Roman clothes copied Greek styles, but new fashions were often influenced by costumes from conquered regions.

The ankle-length *tunica talaris* had long, fitted sleeves and was often brightly decorated. It was worn by both men and women.

Tunic styles

During the republic, men of all **ranks** wore tunics like Greek *chitons*. They were usually short, and did not have sleeves. In the empire, men generally wore short, T-shaped tunics with sleeves. They were often made of linen and decorated with two vertical stripes, or with **tapestry** panels. Later, the full-length *tunica talaris* (see left) and long, wide-sleeved *dalmatica* came into fashion.

Toga types

Men often wore togas over their tunics. A toga was made by draping a large semicircle of woolen cloth around the body. In imperial times, only Roman citizens were allowed to wear togas. There were several types of toga. The plain *toga virilis* was woven from undyed wool and was worn by adult men. The *toga praetexta*, which had a purple border along the straight edge, was worn by boys under 16 and by some officials.

Roman boys wore a necklace called a *bulla* to protect them from evil. Sometimes it was made of a golden ball with a charm inside. Poor boys made *bullas* from a long strip of leather tied in a knot.

Stolas and pallas

The main item of female clothing during the republic was the *stola*. This was a robe like a long *chiton*, with or without sleeves. A rectangular cloak called a *palla* was draped over it. Both garments were still worn under the empire, and long tunics also became popular. During this period, women's clothing became more richly decorated.

This simple type of Roman shoe is called a *carbatina*. It was made from one piece of leather wrapped around the foot. The shoe was held in place with a leather tie around the ankle.

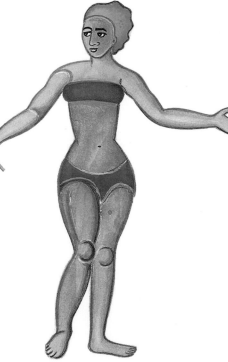

This drawing is based on a Roman **mosaic**. The woman is wearing a breast band and a short, fitted loincloth made of linen or leather. These garments were probably the underclothes worn by most Roman women.

From Tebenna to Toga

The Etruscans lived in central Italy from about the eighth century BC on, and were eventually conquered by the Romans. They may have originally come from Turkey, and their clothing was influenced by both Asian and Greek styles. The Etruscans often wore a draped garment called a *tebenna* over a tunic (see right). The *tebenna* was the ancestor of the Roman toga.

MATERIAL MATTERS

The Romans wove wool and linen to make their garments, and brought cotton from India and silk from China. They also made a special fabric called *cilicium* from goats' hair. It was waterproof, so fishermen often wore *cilicium* clothing when they went out in their boats.

IMPERIAL STYLE C. 100 AD

The man on the right is wearing a short-sleeved tunic called a *tunica laticlavia*. This special type of tunic was worn only by **senators**. The tunic has two vertical tapestry stripes running from shoulder to hem, back and front. They have been colored using a dye from a shellfish called murex. Over the top of the tunic the man wears a *toga virilis*, made of undyed wool. The fabric is draped simply, over the left shoulder, around the back and under the right arm, finishing at the shoulder again. In later years, togas were draped in more complex ways. From about the third century AD on, togas were usually worn only for grand ceremonies.

The woman on the left is dressed in a *stola* with sleeves. It is made of fine linen. Her woolen *palla* is draped over one shoulder and pulled up over her head. The woman's hair is pulled into a **chignon** at the back, and at the front she has three rows of artificial curls.

SOLDIERS IN ANCIENT ROME

The Romans conquered a huge empire thanks to their large, disciplined army. During the rule of the first emperor, Augustus, the army became a permanent, professional fighting force. Imperial soldiers, called legionaries, went to war dressed in metal armor and carrying short swords, spears and shields.

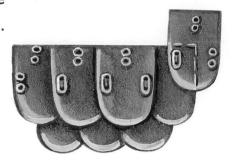

Body armor

Legionaries protected their chests and backs with various forms of body armor—**chain mail** made of linked metal rings, **scale armor** made of overlapping metal plates, or the *lorica segmentata* (see far right). Leather straps protected shoulders, necks and thighs. Underneath their armor legionaries wore short tunics made of wool with short sleeves. In cold regions, they also wore half-length or full-length trousers called *braccae*, and often a thick, red woolen cloak called a *sagum*. Men tucked scarves into their armor at the neck to keep it from rubbing the skin.

Helmet styles

The earliest helmets were made of leather, but this was later replaced by metal, often decorated with feathers or horsehair crests. By the time of the **empire**, plain bronze or iron helmets were more common, although some officers wore helmets with crests. Imperial helmets had cheek- and neck-flaps to protect these areas.

Soldiers' shoes

Marching and fighting were hard on the feet, so Roman legionaries wore strong leather sandals called *caligae* or short, laced-up boots, some with animal-skin linings. The soles had nails in them to make them more hard-wearing. Officers protected their lower legs with metal **greaves**.

Roman army officers called centurions wore helmets with crests running from side to side rather than front to back.

Centurions carried special staffs (sticks) made of vine wood. They used them to beat legionaries as part of their training or to punish disobedience.

The small metal plates that made up Roman scale armor were joined together one by one. Then they were attached to a fabric lining. This was probably made of roughly woven linen.

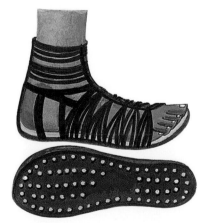

Both foot and cavalry soldiers wore sandals like this, known as *caligae*. They were made of leather and had nails in the soles.

FIGHTING FASHIONS c.150 AD.

The legionary shown here is wearing the *lorica segmentata* over his tunic and short *braccae* trousers. This type of armor was made of steel strips attached to a leather lining and fastened with buckles and leather ties. It allowed soldiers to move more freely than other types of back- and breastplate. An apron of metal-plated leather strips hangs from the soldier's belt. On his right is a wooden shield, painted blue and decorated with a thunderbolt. He carries a throwing spear called a *pilum* in his left hand.

The other soldier is a standard-bearer. His job was to carry the standard (emblem) of a century (a group of 80 legionaries) into battle. He is holding a standard and wearing chain-mail armor over his woolen tunic. He has an animal skin draped over his helmet.

MATERIAL MATTERS

The army used so much material for its uniforms that in the third century AD the government set up mills to produce all the wool that it needed. The mills also supplied fabric for government officials' clothes.

Gladiator Armor

A gladiator was someone trained to fight in public to entertain an audience. There were four types of gladiator. Each type had its own style of armor. Samnite gladiators (see left) wore metal helmets with **visors** and short wool or linen **kilts** that were cut high at the side of the legs. The lower halves of their legs were protected by metal greaves, and their right arms and left thighs were also armored.

THE CELTS

This bronze helmet with pointed horns was probably made in the first century BC. It belonged to a Celtic chieftain, but he may have worn it for special ceremonies rather than for battle.

Experts are unsure when the people known as the Celts arrived in central Europe, but they were settled there by about 800 BC. Slowly they spread into Spain, Portugal, Britain and Ireland. The Romans defeated the Celts of mainland Europe and Britain in the first centuries BC and AD. From then on, the two peoples greatly influenced each other's costume styles.

From woad to wool

The early Celts wore little except furs. They also painted a blue dye called woad on their skin. Later, they learned to weave wool and to make simple clothes. Men wore short tunics, with short or long sleeves, and trousers. Women dressed in long gowns. The tunics and gowns were often belted at the waist. Both men and women wore large cloaks, which they also used as blankets.

The Celts were skillful metalworkers. They made this finely decorated torque from a metal called electrum, which is a mixture of gold and silver.

Military dress

While fighting for themselves and later as part of the Roman armies, Celtic warriors dressed in a variety of garments. These included tunics, cloaks, **chain mail** armor and horned helmets. They wore neck rings called torques, made of metals such as gold, and carried decorated metal shields. Some warriors tattooed woad patterns on their faces, arms and legs.

The Celts knew how to make glass. They made rings of different colors by adding minerals to the glass mixture.

Celtic colors

The Celts loved bright colors and often dyed wool before it was made into clothing. Many plants and fruits were used to make the dyes. The wools were then used to weave patterns. Checks were popular, but circles, stripes and other designs were also common. Patchwork bands were sometimes added to finished garments.

Roman Influence

Romans sometimes wore Celtic-style trousers and cloaks. In the same way, rich Celts in Roman Britain often wore Roman-style tunics and cloaks, though not togas. A hooded cloak called a *birrus* (see right) was especially popular among Celts under Roman rule in both Britain and France. The cloak was made of thick, coarse, undyed wool and eventually developed into the hooded habit worn by many Christian monks.

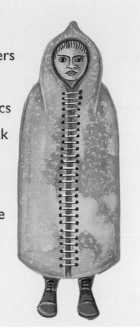

MATERIAL MATTERS
Poor Celts continued to wear tunics and trousers made of goatskin long after weaving was invented. The rich, both men and women, sometimes put simple fur vests over woven garments, and men sometimes draped animal-skin capes around their shoulders for warmth.

CELTIC CHECKS C. 100 AD

This family group is dressed in typical Celtic style. The man wears trousers made of checked wool. They are held up around the waist by a cord and tied tight around the ankles. His shoes are made of leather with the fur still attached and worn on the inside. Most Celtic men had long hair and a drooping mustache as shown here.

The woman in the group is wearing an ankle-length belted gown. She has a cloak of checked wool fastened around her shoulders with a bronze clasp called a **fibula**. Her hair is long and braided, and her eyebrows are dyed black with berry juice. Her child wears a short tunic belted at the waist.

THE MIGRATING TRIBES

The Romans brought the Celts (see pages 30–31) under their control, but by the fourth century AD other peoples threatened their **empire**. They included Asiatic tribes from the east, such as the Huns, and Germanic tribes from the north, such as the Franks. All these peoples wore some form of trousers and short tunics.

This Hun is wearing a leather skullcap with a fur border. Hats like this were ideal for the cold climate of central Asia.

Hun style

The Huns came from the cold **steppes** of central Asia. They were skilled horsemen who wore close-fitting trousers and short-sleeved tunics of rough linen, belted at the waist. They had cloaks of fur or cloth, fastened around the neck, sometimes with brooches. The Huns were a fierce people who cared little for how they looked. They wore their garments until they fell apart.

Members of many tribes sometimes fought with the Roman armies instead of against them. They often wore simple tunics and trousers instead of metal armor. Their main weapons were shields, swords and spears.

The Franks

Early Frankish warriors, from western Germany, often wore legging-style trousers bound on with strips of cloth. These were sometimes worn with a short-sleeved fitted top, but could also be joined to a vest, forming a kind of all-in-one suit. Like the Celts, the Franks wore simple leather shoes with the fur on the inside.

The Goths

The Germanic Goths lived around the Black Sea until the Huns pushed them west. At first they wore trousers and long-sleeved linen tunics with fur borders, but later they also dressed in the **chain mail** armor and metal helmets of the Romans. On their feet they wore short leather boots. A group of Goths called the Visigoths captured and sacked Rome in 410 AD.

The Lombards were a Germanic tribe who invaded Italy during the sixth century AD. This engraved figure shows a Lombard horseman wearing a decorated tunic and plain leggings.

32

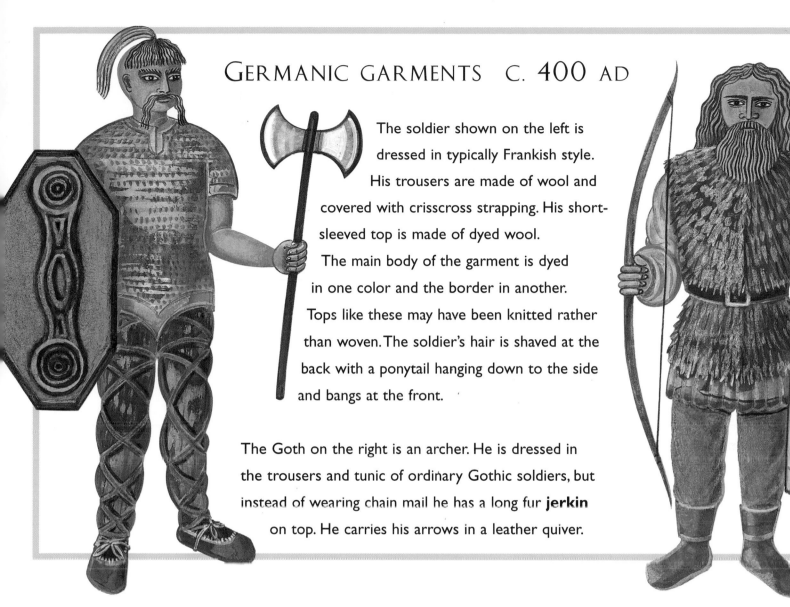

GERMANIC GARMENTS C. 400 AD

The soldier shown on the left is dressed in typically Frankish style. His trousers are made of wool and covered with crisscross strapping. His short-sleeved top is made of dyed wool. The main body of the garment is dyed in one color and the border in another. Tops like these may have been knitted rather than woven. The soldier's hair is shaved at the back with a ponytail hanging down to the side and bangs at the front.

The Goth on the right is an archer. He is dressed in the trousers and tunic of ordinary Gothic soldiers, but instead of wearing chain mail he has a long fur **jerkin** on top. He carries his arrows in a leather quiver.

MATERIAL MATTERS

Some Germanic tribes, including the Teutons, made many of their clothes from the plant called **hemp**. They wove its fibers into a cloth. Hemp is a material used to produce rope, so the garments were probably rough and scratchy.

Gothic Jewels

The Goths made beautiful jewelry from precious metals, pearls and jewels such as garnets. The Visigoths continued this tradition when they set up a kingdom in Spain during the sixth century. This beautiful cross was discovered in their capital city, Toledo.

ANCIENT INDIA AND PAKISTAN

One of the world's first civilizations grew up in Pakistan's Indus Valley in about 2500 BC. The people who lived there dressed in loincloths. Similar simple garments were worn in the Indian **subcontinent** for the whole ancient period.

Clothes in the Indus Valley

There is little evidence to show what Indus Valley people wore. One surviving statue is of a man wearing a shawl, armlet and headband. He was probably a priest-king, so his garments are not typical. Ancient figurines suggest that ordinary men and women wore cotton loincloths. Women may have worn **girdles** around their waists, too.

Aryan attire

In about 1500 BC, the people known as Aryans settled in northern India. No images of their clothing have survived, but many items are mentioned in the Hindu scriptures, called the Vedas. Experts believe that people of this era wore a long, skirtlike garment that hung down from the waist in pleats. They probably also draped a piece of cloth over the upper body in various ways. Gold and silver jewelry were common.

Mauryan modes

The Mauryan dynasty ruled India from the fourth to the second century BC, and statues from the end of this era have survived. They show men in long *dhoti* (loincloths) with **kamarband** waistbands. Women are shown in similar garments draped lower on the waist. This style of clothing was worn over the following centuries, altering slightly under new dynasties such as the Guptas (see right). There were no major changes in costume until Muslims conquered parts of India in the eleventh century.

This statue was found in the Indus Valley city of Mohenjo-daro. It is more than 4,000 years old and shows a bearded priest-king. The man's shawl is patterned and draped over his left shoulder.

Women probably began to wear the *bindi* mark on their foreheads in Gupta times. It may have been a sign that they were married.

This necklace and bracelet were also discovered at Mohenjo-daro. The beads are made of **carnelian**, gold, baked clay and **soapstone**.

Tying Turbans

Turbans are mentioned in the Hindu scriptures, and in very ancient times both men and women wore them. By the second century BC they were a standard part of men's dress. They were fastened with a large knot at the front. A lock of hair was usually tied into the knot.

MATERIAL MATTERS

The people of the Indus Valley were the first in the world to grow cotton and to turn it into fabric. They made dyes from the plants of the region and used them to dye the fabric many bright colors before making their garments.

CHANGING STYLES C. 200 BC–1400 AD

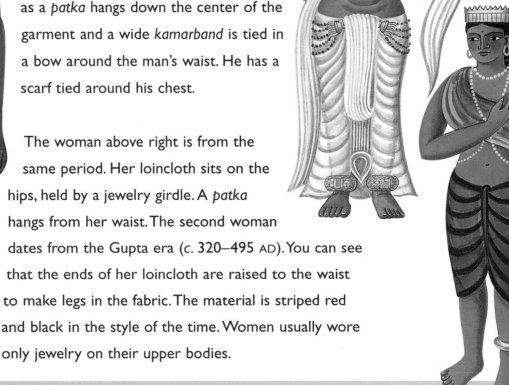

The man shown on the left is wearing clothes from about 200 BC, during the Mauryan era. His loincloth has been pulled up at the overlap to create a V shape between the legs. A strip of embroidered cloth known as a *patka* hangs down the center of the garment and a wide *kamarband* is tied in a bow around the man's waist. He has a scarf tied around his chest.

The woman above right is from the same period. Her loincloth sits on the hips, held by a jewelry girdle. A *patka* hangs from her waist. The second woman dates from the Gupta era (c. 320–495 AD). You can see that the ends of her loincloth are raised to the waist to make legs in the fabric. The material is striped red and black in the style of the time. Women usually wore only jewelry on their upper bodies.

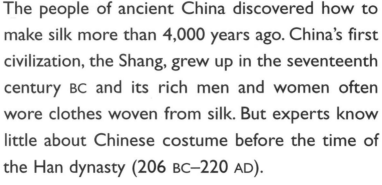

c. 17th century–1027 BC
Shang dynasty rules China.

c. 1027–256 BC
Period of Chou dynasty.

551–479 BC
Life of Chinese
philosopher Confucius.

221–207 BC
Period of Qin dynasty.

ANCIENT CHINA

The people of ancient China discovered how to make silk more than 4,000 years ago. China's first civilization, the Shang, grew up in the seventeenth century BC and its rich men and women often wore clothes woven from silk. But experts know little about Chinese costume before the time of the Han dynasty (206 BC–220 AD).

Flowing robes

In the Han era, wealthy people often wore a flowing, floor-length *p'ao robe*. The two sides of the robe crossed over at the front and were tied with a **girdle** at the waist. The robes were usually made of plain or patterned silk, sometimes embroidered in gold or trimmed with fur.

Trousers and jackets

Trousers were also common garments for men and women, especially the poor. A knee-length jacket was often worn on top, tied at the waist. These items were made of rough **hemp**, cotton or other fabrics, depending on the wearer's wealth and the climate. Padding was added for warmth. Poor people sometimes wore shoes made of cloth or straw, but usually they went barefoot.

Military costume

In the period just before the Han dynasty, China was united by Emperor Shi Huang Di. When he died in 210 BC, the emperor was buried in a tomb protected by an army of 7,000 life-size clay warriors. They are modeled to look as if they are dressed in armor, or in cloth trousers and tunics. Like Roman soldiers, they have scarves around their necks to prevent their armor from rubbing. This **Terra-cotta** Army gives experts plenty of evidence for military costume in ancient China.

This ancient Chinese emperor is wearing a special style of flat hat that was probably made of stiffened black silk. It has rows of beads hanging down in front of the eyes and behind the head.

A pair of shoes like these were found in a Han dynasty tomb. They are made of silk and were held on the feet with silk ties.

The warriors of the Terra-cotta Army are very detailed. On many of them you can even see the rivets that held the iron squares of their armor together.

36

MATERIAL MATTERS

According to legend, a silkworm cocoon (see below) once dropped into hot tea that the ancient Chinese empress Hsi-Ling was drinking. At once the cocoon's long, shiny fibers unraveled and the empress realized that a fabric could be made from them. This story is probably not true, but the Chinese did develop a silk industry in the far-distant past. They grew orchards of mulberry trees for the silkworms to feed on, waited until they made their cocoons, then unwound, spooled and wove the fibers.

The Silk Roads

The Chinese kept the process of silk-making secret for thousands of years. So Romans and other foreigners who wanted silk **yarn** or fabric had to buy it from them. Trade routes from China through central Asia to the West reached the **Roman Empire** by the first century They were called the **Silk Roads**, although camel caravans also carried other goods along them. The secret of cultivating the silkworm was finally discovered in the West by about the fifth century AD.

RICH AND POOR c. 100 AD

The wealthy man on the left is wearing a full *p'ao* robe made of red silk with a design in the weave. His sleeves are wide and hang in loose folds from his wrists. The man's silk slippers, tied on with ribbons, can just be seen under the hem of the *p'ao*. He has a cap made from cleverly folded black silk perched on his head.

The poor man on the right is dressed in a short, padded jacket with elbow-length sleeves. His wide trousers finish below the knee. He has cloth shoes tied around his ankles and a rough cloth hat on his head.

THE ANCIENT AMERICAS

During the last **Ice Age** a land bridge linked North America to Asia. Humans crossed over it into the Americas between 40,000 and 12,000 years ago. By 300 AD, the Maya civilization was at its height in Guatemala and Mexico. Many peoples also settled further north.

A backstrap loom had a strap at one end that was worn around the weaver's back. Another strap at the front of the loom was tied around a post or tree. Weavers sat back so that the cloth they were making was pulled tight.

Colorful cloth

The Maya made clothing of light materials suitable for their hot climate. Important members of society dressed in cotton, woven on backstrap **looms**. Feathers or rabbit fur were sometimes woven into the cotton for warmth. Poor people made clothes from tree bark. Woven sisal (see far right) was also used. The Maya loved color and decoration. They stained cloth with plant dyes and decorated clothing with embroidery, shells and beads.

The Adena people lived in southeastern North America from about 1000 BC. They made burial mounds for the dead, and put carvings in them like this one. It shows a man wearing a patterned loincloth. He also has huge disks in his ears.

Maya costume

Maya men usually wore a loincloth. Women wore a long wraparound skirt with a **poncho** (*quechquemitl*) or a tunic (*huipil*) over the top. Ordinary men and women wore cloaks made of cloth. The rich wore feather or jaguar-skin cloaks. The Maya decorated themselves with **jade**, shell and other jewelry. They also wore feather headdresses. Maya soldiers wore tunics made of tough **tapir hide**.

This Maya man is wearing a jaguar skin. The jaguar's head is perched on top of his head, and jaguar-skin bands decorate his feet.

North American variety

Many peoples made their homes in North America. Their clothing depended on local materials and climate. In the far north, they dressed in furs and sealskin boots. Peoples of the northwest Pacific coast probably wore capes of woven cedar bark and blankets of goat hair. In the woodlands of the northeast, men and women dressed in deerskin decorated with porcupine quills.

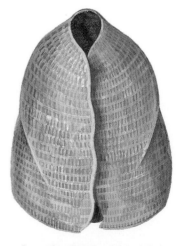

A cedar-bark cape of the type made on the northwest coast of North America. These garments were often trimmed with the fur of sea otters.

FEATHERY FASHIONS C. 400 AD

The Maya woman on the left is wearing a plain wraparound skirt made of loosely woven cotton. Her fringed *quechquemitl* has been colored using natural dyes. The woman also wears a feathered headdress and decorated leather armbands.

The Maya man on the right is wearing a loincloth. The fabric is pulled up between the legs, tucked in at the waist and left to hang in loops. Around his neck he wears shell beads. The man's headdress includes the tail feathers of tropical birds. On his feet he is wearing leather sandals that are closed at the back and open at the front. He also has leather bands on his legs.

Dressed for Success

Pacal was a seventh-century ruler of the Maya city of Palenque in Mexico. He wore water lilies in his hair and tied it up to look like the crest feathers of a macaw. His head was pointed, because it had been bound when he was a baby to show that he was a member of Maya royalty.

MATERIAL MATTERS

Sisal is a type of flowering plant with thick, juicy leaves that grows in Mexico. The Maya used its tough fibers to weave material for clothing.

Today sisal is mainly used for rope-making. The Maya also wove smooth cloth from other plant fibers, such as yucca.

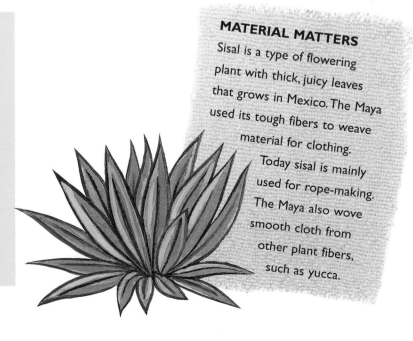

MATERIAL MATTERS

Here you can find out more about the most important clothing materials featured on earlier pages. They are animal furs and skins, and the four most widely used ancient textiles—linen, wool, cotton and silk.

A flax plant in full flower. The plants grow almost 3 feet tall.

Animal furs and skins

Furs and skins were used to make the first garments in many parts of the world. Many animals, such as reindeer and caribou in Europe and jaguars in South America, were hunted for their fur coats. Often the hair was removed and the skins were **tanned** to make leather. This could then be turned into clothes and shoes. **Archaeologists** have discovered ancient robes in Asia that are made of squirrel fur and **sable hides**.

Early peoples often stretched and dried animal skins by attaching them to frames made of wooden sticks.

Harvested stalks of flax

Linen

Linen was probably the first textile ever (see page 8). It was made from the stems of **flax** plants. The stems were dried, then soaked (retted) to separate the hard parts from the fibers suitable for spinning. The spun fibers were then woven into cloth. The whole process is shown in ancient Egyptian tomb paintings. Linen clothing was especially popular in Egypt, where strips of linen were used to wrap mummies too. Linen was also worn in the Middle East, Turkey and parts of Europe.

A Soay sheep. Some of the earliest woolen clothes in Europe were probably made from the fleeces of sheep like this. Their coats have several different colors in them and are made up of hair as well as wool.

Flax stalks before (top) and after retting. This process causes bacteria to break down the hard parts of the flax. The soft fibers suitable for clothmaking can then be removed.

Wool

Wool is probably the second oldest fabric (see page 8). Woolen cloth was first produced when people in Mesopotamia and Egypt started to herd flocks of sheep. At first, the sheep's fleeces were plucked out, but later metal cutting tools were invented, and farmers sheared their flocks. The fleeces were combed, cleaned and spun

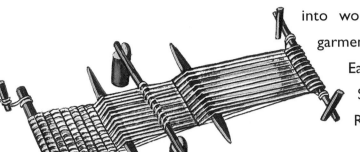

The early ancient Egyptians used ground looms (above) for weaving. Later, they developed upright looms. These were also used in ancient Europe. The peoples of South and Central America often wove their textiles on backstrap looms (see page 38).

into wool thread, which was woven into garments. Goat wool was used in the Middle East, and llama wool was common in South America. The Greeks and Romans wore fine sheep's wool.

Cotton

Cotton was first planted and harvested in India and Pakistan (see page 8), but it was also grown in ancient China, Mesopotamia, Egypt and the Americas. Alexander the Great (see page 25) brought cotton plants to Europe from India in the fourth century BC, but the Greeks and Romans continued to wear wool and linen far more than cotton. The textile is produced by picking fluffy, white **bolls** off the plants (see right), carefully removing the seeds, then spinning and weaving the boll fibers.

Silk

Silk is made from silkworm cocoons (see below). It was first made in China between 4,000 and perhaps as many as 7,000 years ago (see page 37). The secret of silkmaking spread to Korea and Japan in about the third century AD. Then it moved west along the **Silk Roads** to central Asia, Persia, Syria and finally Europe in the first to fourth centuries AD. Before this date, the Greeks and Romans imported silk from China as silk fiber, or as clothing, which they unpicked and wove into their own fashions.

Cotton plants grow up to 8 feet tall. They produce flowers like this.

After the cotton flowers fall off, seed pods called bolls develop.

A Silkworms are the caterpillars of silk moths. Each worm feeds on mulberry leaves before settling on a twig to build a cocoon.

B The sticky silk threads come out of a hole in the silkworm's head. The worm surrounds itself with more and more of them.

C After about three days, the cocoon is complete. The worm is now surrounded by about 900 feet of glossy fibers ready to be unraveled.

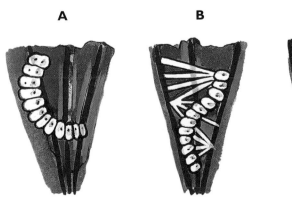

A   B   C

The bolls grow to about the size of eggs, then burst open to show their seeds. The seeds are surrounded by fluffy white cotton fibers known as lint (above). Before the fibers can be spun, the seeds have to be removed.

ANCIENT ACCESSORIES

To complete their costumes, ancient people wore all sorts of accessories. Some, for example glittering necklaces, were mainly for decoration. Others, for example hard-wearing army boots, had a practical purpose. You have already read about some of these items earlier in this book. This chart tells you more, and makes it easy to compare the jewelry, footwear and headgear worn at many times and in many places.

	JEWELRY	FOOTWEAR	HEADGEAR
PREHISTORIC TIMES	30,000 years ago—the first jewelry is made of bone, stone and **ivory**. 10,000 years ago—**amber** is popular. 6,000 years ago—**jade** and gold (from gold nuggets found in rivers) are introduced.	First humans go barefoot. In cold regions shoes are made from animal furs tied around the feet. People learn to sew, and make shoes and boots. **Moccasins** are made from skins with the fur removed.	People go bareheaded in hot regions. Fur caps are worn in cold areas. Some tunics have fur hoods. People sometimes wear special headdresses for religious rituals.
MESOPOTAMIA	Sumerians make jewelry from gold, pearls and gems such as **carnelian** and **lapis lazuli**. Babylonians and Assyrians use gold for heavy armbands and earrings, and delicate hair **fillets** often set with gems.	Mesopotamian peoples generally wear leather sandals with straps at the front and a covered heel at the back. Soldiers usually wear knee-length leather boots tied with laces.	Women pull shawls over their heads. Babylonian and Assyrian kings wear high headdresses. Babylonian men have skullcaps with brims or (like the Assyrians) tall hats.
ANCIENT EGYPT	Egyptians make gold and silver jewelry set with stones such as lapis lazuli and turquoise. Collars, **pectorals** and bracelets are popular. Decorative patterns include **lotus flowers** and **scarab beetles**.	Ancient Egyptians often go barefoot, but sandals are also common. These are made of woven palm leaves, **papyrus** or leather. Most have a thong that separates the big toe and the second toe.	Pharaohs wear a red-and-white double crown, a striped linen headcloth called a *nemes*, or a headdress. Queens wear headdresses—one style is shaped like a bird. Ordinary women wear headbands.
HEBREWS	Hebrews often wear gold jewelry, including bracelets and chain necklaces. Some sprinkle gold dust on their hair. Women wear earrings, and some wear veils with coins or jewels along the edges.	Strapped leather sandals are common. Some people may wear shoes with upturned toes. Women in cities sometimes put **pattens** over their shoes to protect them from mud in the streets.	Hebrew men wear soft caps or turbans. From the early centuries AD, men drape cloaks over their heads for prayer. Early Hebrew women pull cloaks over their hair. By the early centuries AD they wear veils.
PERSIA	Persians copy Assyrian jewelry styles. Pieces are made of gold and often carved with animal designs. Some include mythical creatures such as griffins, which have the head of an eagle and body of a lion.	Persians wear leather shoes fastened with ties or buttons (styles developed from horse-riding ancestors). Baggy leather boots with small heels are also worn, especially by **cavalry** soldiers.	There is a wide range of Persian headwear. Phrygian caps are popular among ordinary men. Kings usually wear gold and jeweled crowns. Soldiers wear hats and helmets. Women are often veiled.

JEWELRY	FOOTWEAR	HEADGEAR	
Minoans wear elaborate bracelets and necklaces of gold, silver or bronze. Women wear spiral-shaped metal earrings and pearl hair decorations. Mycenaeans use gold for **diadem** crowns and other items.	Minoans and Mycenaeans often go barefoot. Leather sandals, often with straps winding up the leg, are also common. Men sometimes wear leather boots or wind strips of cloth around their lower legs.	Men in Crete and Mycenae usually go bareheaded. Sometimes they wear simple, beret-style caps. Women have a variety of ornate tall hats, but probably for ceremonial wear only.	CRETE AND MYCENAE
Women wear delicate jewelry. Many items are decorated with twisted gold wire or set with **enamel**. People fasten clothing with *fibula* pins. Men wear little jewelry, other than rings.	Men and women usually go barefoot. There are also boots, shoes and strapped sandals made of soft calf or tough cow leather. Sandals often have nails in the soles. Some spell out words such as "Follow me."	Men wear felt hats, such as the *petasos*. Women pull cloaks over their heads. In later years women wear brimmed, pointed hats called *tholia*, probably made of straw. Soldiers wear various types of helmet.	ANCIENT GREECE
Women wear several pieces of jewelry, including necklaces, bracelets and earrings. The finest are made of gems set in gold. **Cameos** are popular. Men wear rings only. Boys wear protective *bulla* necklaces.	Men and women wear a variety of leather sandals, shoes and boots. The *crepida* closes like a shoe over the heel, but has straps on top. Soldiers wear sandals called *caligae* or closed-in boots.	Men and women usually go bareheaded. Women also pull up their cloaks over their heads. Some cloaks have hoods. Women also wear veils and tie ribbons around their hair or cover it with pearl-decorated nets.	ANCIENT ROME
Celts make jewelry from gold, silver, other metals and glass. The torque neck ring is worn by important men and women. People fasten their clothing with decorated *fibula* pins.	Celts in Britain wear leather shoes with fur left on the inside for warmth. Celts in France, known as Gauls, wear leather sandals. Under Roman rule, many Celts wear Roman styles of footwear.	Celts generally use cloaks to cover their heads. In France, women may wear broad-brimmed hats made of felt. Men also own horned battle helmets, but these may be for ceremonial use only.	CELTS
Goths and other peoples who migrate into the **Roman Empire** often wear Roman jewelry styles. Later, the Visigoths in Spain make new styles of jewelry, buckles and other items from gold and gems.	Migrating tribes have a variety of simple leather shoes with fur left on the inside. Short leather boots are worn, especially by fighting men. Boots are sometimes pulled tight around the ankles with laces.	Many people go bareheaded. Hunnish men wear warm, fur-trimmed skullcaps. In battle, Goths and others begin to wear strong metal helmets, copied from those worn by Roman soldiers.	MIGRATING TRIBES
Women of the Indus Valley wear metal bracelets and necklaces, and **girdles** made of stones such as jade and carnelian. Guptas wear diamonds, cut into shape so that they sparkle in the light.	Men and women of India and Pakistan usually go barefoot. Women wear toe rings and chains or metal hoops around their ankles. Sometimes the hoops are so heavy women find it difficult to walk.	Until the 2nd century BC turbans are worn by men and women, but then become garments for men only. Women sometimes wear circlets with two ribbons hanging down at the back, or simple diadems.	ANCIENT INDIA AND PAKISTAN
The Chinese prefer silver jewelry to gold, but sometimes put a thin layer of gold on top to prevent the metal from discoloring (it goes black in the air). Jade is a favorite stone. It is imported from central Asia.	Rich men and women wear silk or silk-lined leather slippers. Some are fastened on with ribbons. The poor make their footwear from natural materials such as straw and rushes, or from pieces of cloth.	Rich Chinese men wear hats made of folded silk or other cloth. Some are decorated with beads. The different hat styles of officials show their **rank**. Women wear jeweled combs in their hair.	ANCIENT CHINA
Maya wear heavy earrings, armbands and **pendants**. Jade is the most popular stone. Jewelry is also made of tropical bird feathers. The Adena people of North America make copper bracelets and rings.	Maya often go barefoot, but also wear simple leather sandals or moccasins. Many early North American peoples also go barefoot. In the cold northeast and northwest, moccasins are popular.	Maya often wear headdresses made of brightly colored feathers. In northwestern North America, people weave hats from tree roots or bark. In the southeast, eagle feathers are used as hair decorations.	THE ANCIENT AMERICAS

43

MAPS OF THE ANCIENT WORLD

Many of the empires, countries, regions and cities of the ancient world were known by names that we no longer use. The maps on these pages will help you to locate where they were. The world map shows the area that each of the three more detailed maps cover.

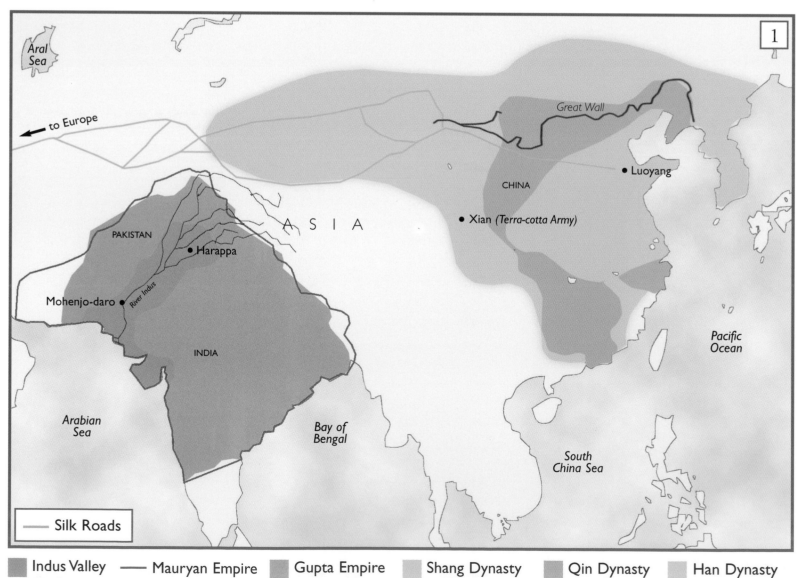

Silk Roads

■ Indus Valley Civilization	— Mauryan Empire c. 381–185 BC	■ Gupta Empire c. 320–495 AD	■ Shang Dynasty c. 17th century –1027 BC	■ Qin Dynasty 221–207 BC	■ Han Dynasty 206 BC–220 AD

The three detailed maps on these pages show:
1. Asia
2. North and Central America
3. Europe, the Middle East, North Africa and western Asia.

They include places that existed at different times during the period covered by this book. Some modern country names have been included, to help you find your way around. The main pages of the book, and the time strips that run along the tops of the pages, will tell you exactly when each played a major part in world history.

General key to place names

EUROPE   Continent name
GREECE   Country name
ASSYRIA   Region or empire name
Babylon   City name

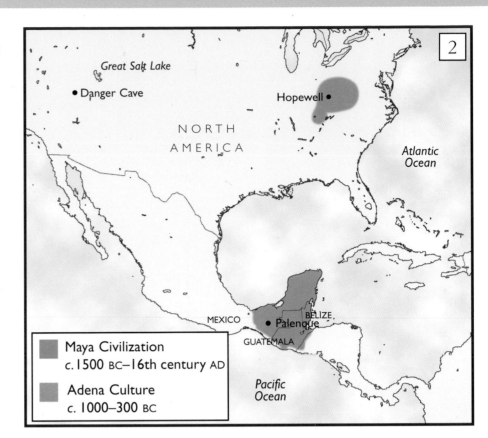

2

- Danger Cave
- Hopewell

NORTH AMERICA

Great Salt Lake

Atlantic Ocean

MEXICO
GUATEMALA
BELIZE
- Palenque

Pacific Ocean

■ Maya Civilization
c.1500 BC–16th century AD

■ Adena Culture
c.1000–300 BC

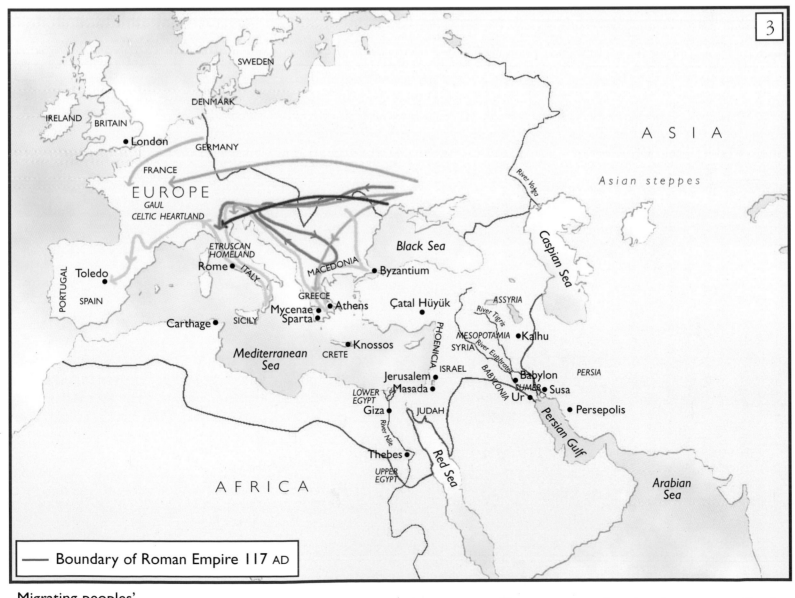

3

SWEDEN
DENMARK
IRELAND
BRITAIN
- London
GERMANY
FRANCE
EUROPE
GAUL
CELTIC HEARTLAND
PORTUGAL
- Toledo
SPAIN
ETRUSCAN HOMELAND
Rome • *ITALY*
MACEDONIA
- Byzantium
Black Sea
GREECE
- Mycenae • Athens
- Sparta
- Çatal Hüyük
Carthage • SICILY
Mediterranean Sea
- Knossos
CRETE
PHOENICIA
ASSYRIA
MESOPOTAMIA • Kalhu
River Tigris
SYRIA
ISRAEL
River Euphrates
- Jerusalem
- Masada
LOWER EGYPT
- Giza
JUDAH
BABYLONIA
- Babylon
SUMER
Ur •
- Susa
PERSIA
- Persepolis
River Nile
- Thebes
Red Sea
Persian Gulf
UPPER EGYPT
AFRICA
Arabian Sea
ASIA
Asian steppes
River Volga
Caspian Sea

—— Boundary of Roman Empire 117 AD

Migrating peoples' invasion of Europe   —— Visigoths   —— Ostrogoths   —— Huns   —— Lombards   —— Franks

GLOSSARY

agate A type of gemstone that comes in many colors, including blue and green. It is often striped.

alkaline A word describing an alkali —a substance that neutralizes acids. Some alkalis are so strong that they can dissolve materials such as fur.

alpaca A South American animal that belongs to the camel family. It has long, brown, silky fur.

amber Fossilized resin from extinct, cone-bearing trees. The resin is usually orange, brown or yellow.

apron A type of garment worn by men, for example in Egypt and Crete. Aprons hang down from the waist at the front and cover part of the legs. Some also cover the leg backs.

archaeologist A person who studies the past by digging up old sites and examining old objects.

awl A tool with a sharp point. It is used to make holes in leather and other strong materials.

baldric A sword belt worn across the upper body. The sword hangs down from the baldric at the side.

bodice A tight-fitting garment worn on the upper part of a woman's body. It may be sleeved or sleeveless and is often fastened with laces.

boll A seed pod on a cotton plant.

Bronze Age The period of prehistory during which people made tools from bronze. It followed the Stone Age, but its dates varied from place to place. In Scandinavia, it lasted from about 1800 to 500 BC.

cameo Jewelry made from two different gemstone layers. The top layer was often cut into a face shape.

carnelian A type of orange-red gemstone.

cavalry The part of an army whose soldiers ride horses into battle.

chain mail A type of armor made from linked metal rings.

chignon A hairstyle in which long hair is arranged in a roll or bun at the back of the head.

chiton A type of loose tunic worn in ancient Greece.

conservator A person who looks after ancient fabrics and other objects, for example in a museum.

cuirass A piece of armor, usually made of metal or leather, that covers the wearer's chest and back.

diadem A large, open circle of precious metal worn as a crown.

empire A large area, often including many different countries, that is united under the rule of a single emperor or empress.

enamel A glasslike substance that is made in many colors. Pieces of enamel are often set into metal to make items of jewelry.

fibula A type of metal pin or brooch that was used by Greeks, Romans and others to fasten garments. Some *fibulae* were beautifully decorated.

fillet A ribbon or other band worn in a circle around the head.

flax A blue-flowered plant from whose stalks linen is made.

flint A type of gray-black rock. Prehistoric people often used sharp-edged pieces of flint as tools.

fresco A type of picture made by applying paints to wet plaster.

gall A growth on leaves or twigs caused by insects.

girdle A waist or hip belt, often with ends that hang loose.

greave A piece of armor, usually made of metal or leather, that covers the wearer's lower leg.

hemp An Asian plant from which people made rough cloth.

hide The skin of an animal.

himation A long cloak worn by ancient Greek men and women.

Ice Age Any of several periods of history when much of the Earth was covered with ice. The most recent Ice Age lasted from about 1.6 million to 10,000 years ago.

inlaid Set into a surface, such as metal, wood or ivory.

Inuit A people descended from the first men and women to settle in Alaska and nearby areas thousands of years ago. Many still live there.

ivory The material animal tusks are made of. It was often carved into jewelry or precious objects.

jade A gemstone that occurs in many colors, but especially green.

jerkin A jacket with no collar and no sleeves.

kamarband A type of sash worn around the waist in ancient India.

kilt A length of cloth that wraps around the waist to form a skirt.

lapis lazuli A bright blue gemstone.

lappet wig A style of ancient Egyptian wig divided into separate hanging sections (lappets).

loom A machine used to weave yarn into cloth.

lotus flower The flower of a type of water lily that the ancient Egyptians believed to be holy.

moccasins A simple leather shoe worn by some early American peoples.

mosaic A floor or wall decoration made of pieces of colored glass or stone arranged into patterns.

nomad A person who moves from place to place in search of food.

obelisk A stone pillar that slopes inward from the bottom to the top.

Old Testament The holy writings of the Hebrews that today make up the first part of the Christian Bible.

p'ao robe A long, loose, crossover robe worn in ancient China.

palla A rectangular cloak worn by Roman women.

papyrus A tall, reedlike plant that grows by lakes and rivers in Africa.

patten An overshoe with a high sole, worn over an ordinary shoe to protect it from dirt and water.

pectoral An item of jewelry worn as a chest decoration.

pendants Strips that hang down from the waist of some ancient Egyptian garments. Also objects that hang from a necklace.

poncho A sleeveless cloak that is pulled on over the head.

prehistoric The word that describes history before writing was invented.

rank A person's position in society. If a person was high-ranking, they were important.

republic A country or area with elected rulers and no king, queen or emperor.

Roman Empire The era (27 BC– 476 AD) in which ancient Rome was ruled by emperors. The term also refers to the area that they governed.

sable A small, weasel-like animal from northern Asia with a shiny, dark brown or black coat.

sari A garment formed by wrapping a long piece of cloth around the body. Saris are traditionally worn in India and Pakistan.

scale armor A type of armor made of overlapping plates of iron, bronze or other metal.

scarab beetle A beetle that the ancient Egyptians believed to be holy.

seal A ring or stamp with a picture cut into it. In the past high-ranking people closed letters with a lump of hot wax or clay, then pressed their seal on it to prove it was from them.

senator An important official in the Roman republic and later the empire.

Silk Road One of the ancient trade routes along which silk was carried from China to the West.

sinew A band of strong white material in the body that joins a muscle to a bone.

soapstone A type of soft, gray-green, brown or white stone.

steppe A large, flat area of grass-covered land, usually without trees.

stola A long sleeved or sleeveless robe worn by Roman women.

subcontinent A land area that forms a large part of a continent.

synagogue A building where Jews hold religious services.

tan To treat animal hides with substances containing the chemical tannin. This process turns them into leather and stops them from rotting.

tapestry A way of making textiles by weaving colored threads into a fixed linen backing. Also fabric made using this technique.

tapir A type of animal. The South American tapir has a short, reddish-brown or black coat.

taw To spread salt and other minerals on animal hides. This ancient method of tanning turned hides into white leather.

terracotta A type of reddish clay.

visor A hinged metal flap on the front of a helmet. It can be raised so that the wearer can see clearly, or lowered for protection.

yarn A length of twisted fibers ready to be woven or knitted into cloth.

INDEX

accessories 42-43
actors, Greek 24, 25
Americas 7, 38-39, 43
animal skins 8, 9, 10, 13, 16, 31, 38, 40
aprons 14, 20, 46
armor 15, 24, 25, 28, 29, 30, 32
art evidence 6-7
Aryans 34
Assyrians 10, 11

Babylonians 10
bark 38
birrus cloaks 31
bodices 20, 46
boots and shoes 8, 9, 18, 26, 36, 37
braccae trousers 28, 29

capes 13, 14, 38
Celts 30-31, 43
chain mail 28, 32, 46
China 36-37, 43
chiton tunics 17, 22, 23, 24, 25, 46
cilicium fabric 27
cloaks 16, 17, 22, 23, 25, 26, 27, 28, 31, 46
conservators 7, 46
cotton 35, 41
Crete 20-21, 43
cuirasses 24, 25, 46

dyes 17, 30, 38

Egypt 12-15, 42
Etruscans 27

feathers 38, 39, 43
felt 9
fibulae 22, 23, 31, 46
flax 8, 15, 40, 46
footwear 8, 9, 10, 14, 16, 18, 20, 26, 28, 30, 36, 37, 42, 43
Franks 32, 33
furs 8, 9, 38, 40

Germanic tribes 32-33
gladiators 29
Goths 32, 33, 43
greaves 24, 28, 29, 46
Greece 17, 22-25, 43

hairstyles 6, 11, 19, 21, 23, 27, 31, 33, 35, 39, 43, 46
hats and caps 18, 19, 23, 32, 36, 39
headdresses 11, 14, 15, 18, 21, 23, 35
Hebrews 16-17, 42
helmets 11, 25, 28, 29, 30
hemp 33, 46
hides (skins) 8, 9, 10, 13, 16, 31, 38, 40, 46
himation cloaks 22, 23, 46
hoplites 24, 25
Huns 32

India 34-35, 43
Indus Valley people 34, 35
Inuit people 9, 46

jackets 36
jerkins 33, 46

kaunakès cloth 10, 11
kamarband waistbands 34, 35, 47
kilts 12, 13, 14, 15, 20, 29, 47

linen 8, 13, 15, 23, 25, 40
loincloths 4, 9, 20, 21, 34, 35, 39
Lombards 32
looms 38, 41, 47
lorica segmentata 28, 29

masks 24, 25
materials 40-41
Maya civilization 38, 39, 43
Mesopotamia 10-11, 42
migrating tribes 32-33, 43
military uniforms *see soldiers* and *armor*
Minoan civilization 20
Mycenae 20, 21, 43

nettles 7
North American peoples 38

Pakistan 34-35, 43
palla cloaks 26, 27, 47
p'ao robes 36, 47
peplos tunics 22, 23
Persia 18-19, 42
pharaohs 14-15
ponchos 38, 47
prayer shawl 16
prehistoric times 4, 8-9, 42
priestly clothes 13, 16

queens of Egypt 14, 15

religious dress 4, 9, 13, 16
Rome 26-29, 31, 43

sandals 10, 14, 16, 20, 28, 30, 42-43
scale armor 28, 47
sewing methods 8
shoes *see footwear* and *boots and shoes*
silk 19, 23, 36, 37, 41
Silk Roads 19, 37, 41, 47
sisal 38, 39
skins *see hides*
soldiers 5, 11, 15, 19, 24, 25, 28-29, 30, 32, 33, 36
stola robes 26, 27, 47
Sumerian civilization 10

tanning 13, 40, 47
tassels 16
tawing process 13, 47
tebenna robes 27
Terra-cotta Army 36
togas 4, 26, 27
turbans 35

weaving 11, 41
wigs 11, 12
woad 30
wool 7, 21, 29, 40-41